San Diego Biotech
DIRECTORY

336 companies assorted

from A-to-Z by domain,

mail address and

brief profile

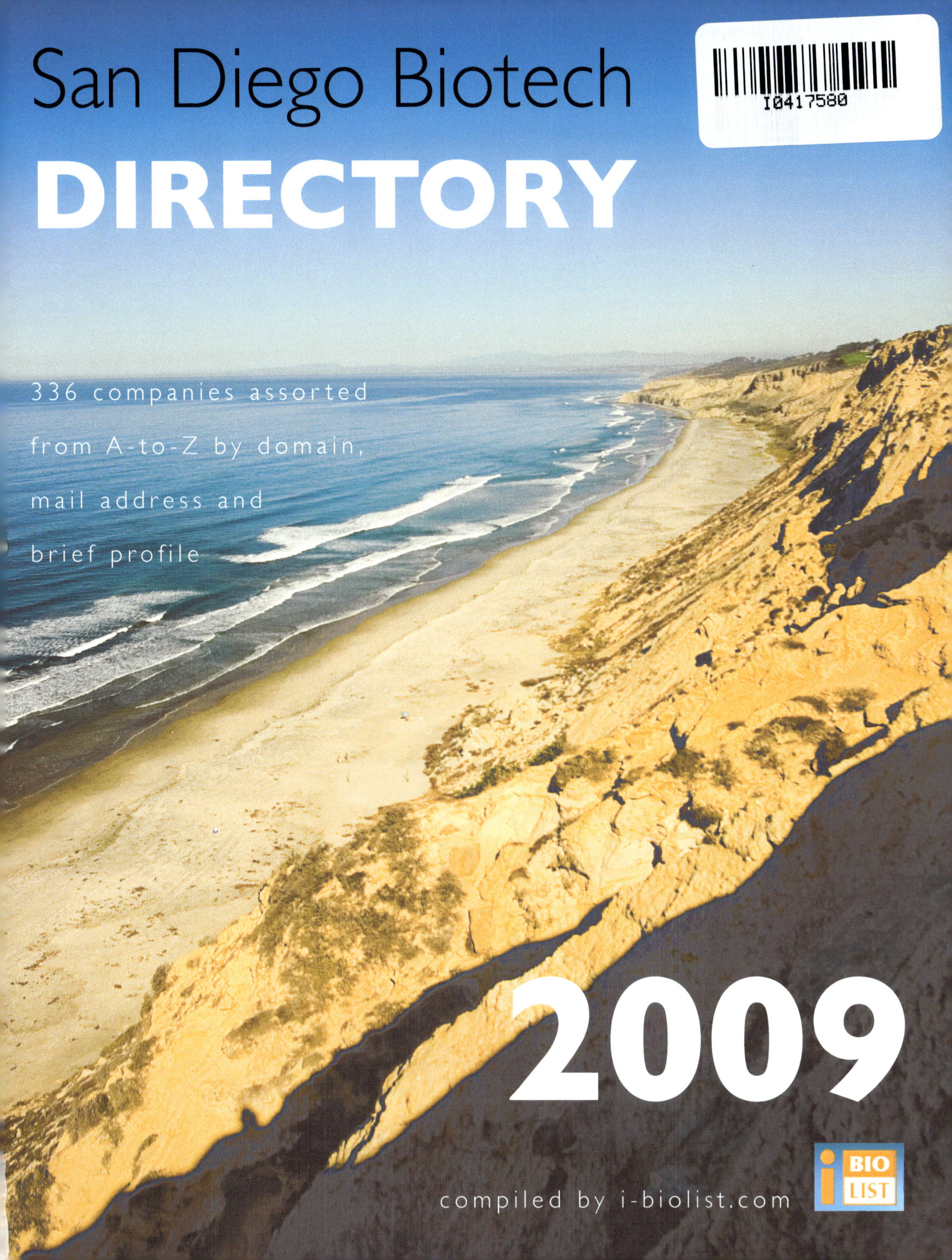

2009

compiled by i-biolist.com

SUMMARY

In the year 2009, the collective focus of the 336 San Diego companies is **research and development**.

Secondary tragets are **drug discovery**, **diseases** and **services**.

Tertiary in importance is the **pharmaceutical** development of **novel anti-cancer therapeutics** followed by **clinical diagnostics**.

see Figure 1 at the end of the PDF document

	COMPANY	ADDRESS	DESCRIPTION
1	www.aaamg.com	6386 Alvarado Court, Suite 210, San Diego, CA, 92120	Allergy Associates Medical Group provides treatment of respiratory and related allergy disorders, such as asthma, allergic rhinitis and sinusitis, urticaria, allergic dermatitis, drug, insect and food allergies.
2	www.abbiotec.com	7955 Dunbrook Road, Suite B, San Diego, CA 92126	Abbiotec is focused on developing and commercializing next generation antibodies and reagents for the life science research community.
3	www.abbottanalytics.com	P.O. Box 22536, San Diego, CA 92192-2536	Abbott Analytics is a leader in applying and integrating data mining methods to marketing, research and business endeavors.
4	www.abgent.com	10239 Flanders Court, San Diego, CA 92121	Abgent develops primary antibodies and provides custom peptide synthesis. The antibodies are used for analysis of autophagy, apoptosis, stem cells, cell function and gene regulation.
5	www.abingdoncorp.com	5963 La Place Ct Suite 107, Carlsbad, CA 92008	Abingdon Life Sciences provides regulatory and clinical support to pharmaceutical and biotech companies in a broad range of areas, including oncology, cardiovascular disease, endocrinology and metabolism, gastroenterology, and infectious diseases.
6	www.acadia-pharm.com	3911 Sorrento Valley Blvd., San Diego, CA 92121 USA	Acadia Pharmaceuticals is a biopharmaceutical company utilizing innovative technology for drug discovery and clinical development of new treatments for central nervous system disorders.
7	www.accelagen.com	6044 Cornerstone Court West, Suite C, San Diego, CA 92121	Accelagen contract services include protein expression and purification.
8	www.accelrys.com	10188 Telesis Court, Suite 100, San Diego, CA 92121	Accelrys develops and commercializes scientific business intelligence software for the integration, mining, modeling and simulation, management and interactive reporting of scientific data.
9	www.accugent.com	5933 Sea Lion Place, Suite 105, Carlsbad, CA 92010	Accugent Laboratories is a contract research organization dedicated to providing analytical, formulation and synthesis services in support of pharmaceutical research and development.
10	www.accumetrics.com	3985 Sorrento Valley Boulevard, San Diego, CA 92121	Accumetrics develops, manufactures, and markets the VerifyNow® System, a comprehensive suite of tests for the assessment of platelet response to antiplatelet therapies.
11	www.aceabio.com	6779 Mesa Ridge Road #100, San Diego, CA 92121	Acea Biosciences has pioneered the development of high-performance microelectronic systems for cell-based assays. Acea and Roche are developing and marketing on a worldwide basis Acea's microplate-based biosensor platform for a variety of applications in drug development, toxicology, cancer research, and medical microbiology and virology.
12	www.aconlab.com	10125 Mesa Rim Road, San Diego, CA 92121	Acon Laboratories provides a broad range of rapid diagnostic and health care products.
13	www.actimis.com	10835 Road To The Cure, Suite 200, San Diego, CA 92121	Actimis Pharmaceuticals is a start-up biopharmaceutical company focused on the development of small molecule therapeutics for respiratory and inflammatory disorders.

	COMPANY	ADDRESS	DESCRIPTION
14	www.activemotif.com	1914 Palomar Oaks Way, Suite 150, Carlsbad, CA 92008	Active Motif is dedicated to developing and delivering innovative cell biology-based research tools and biocomputing resources to help researchers in their quest to study the function, regulation and interactions of the genes and their encoded proteins.
15	www.activx.com	11025 North Torrey Pines Road, Suite 120, La Jolla, CA 92037	ActivX is a biopharmaceutical company that discovers and develops small molecule drugs for major unmet medical needs. ActivX uses its unique technology to identify drug candidates with focus in hematology, oncology, metabolic and inflammatory diseases.
16	www.adnavance.com	11494 Sorrento Valley Road, Suite H, San Diego,CA 92121	The Adnavance patented an ultra-sensitive metalized-DNA (M-DNA™) technology allows to eliminate the need for amplification for a large number of molecular diagnostic tests.
17	www.advancedbiohealing.com	10933 N. Torrey Pines Road, Suite 200, La Jolla, CA 92037	Advanced BioHealing develops and markets cell-based and tissue-engineered products. Products include Dermagraft, a human fibroblast-derived dermal substitute; and TransCyte, a human fibroblast-derived temporary skin substitute, which temporarily covers wound for surgically excised thickness and partial-thickness burns.
18	www.advantarlabs.com	3030 Bunker Hill Dr., Suite 102, San Diego, CA 92109	Advantar Laboratories offers GMP-compliant services including analytical/formulation development, release/stability testing, clinical packaging and strategic consulting.
19	www.adventrx.com	6725 Mesa Ridge Rd., Suite 100, San Diego, CA 92121	Adventrx Pharmaceuticals is a biopharmaceutical research and development company, focused on commercializing proprietary product candidates for the treatment of cancer and infectious diseases.
20	www.aegisthera.com	16870 West Bernardo Drive, Suite 390, San Diego, CA 92127	Aegis Therapeutics is a specialty pharmaceutical company commercializing advanced patented drug delivery and protein stabilization technologies that enable the non-invasive delivery of a broad range of protein, peptide, and non-peptide macromolecular therapeutics.
21	www.aethlonmedical.com	8910 University Center Lane, Suite 255, San Diego, CA 92122	Aethlon Medical has developed a patented extracorporeal device, known as the Hemopurifier®, to address the treatment of viral conditions that are either resistant or evolve resistance to drug and vaccines.
22	www.agscientific.com	8839 Menkar Road, San Diego, CA 92126	A.G. Scientific supplies innovative biochemicals and pharmaceutical raw materials.
23	www.airespharma.com	4690 Executive Drive, Suite 150, San Diego,CA 92121	Aires Pharmaceuticals is a privately-held clinical stage pharmaceutical company developing therapies to treat pulmonary disorders.
24	www.allelebiotech.com	9924 Mesa Rim Road, San Diego, CA 92121	Allele Biotechnology and Pharmaceuticals is a leader in the RNAi field and supplier of fluorescent proteins, highly efficient Luciferase assay substrates, and genotyping kits (all novel products only from Allele).

	COMPANY	ADDRESS	DESCRIPTION
25	www.alliedintrade.com	815 Grand Avenue, Suite 106, San Marcos,CA 92078	Allied Intrade is an American company providing personalized China-based manufacturing services, and logistical management solutions to small US OEMs.
26	www.allp.com	4660 La Jolla Village Drive, Suite 825, San Diego, CA 92122	Alliance Pharmaceutical is a research and development company focused on transforming innovative scientific discoveries into novel therapeutic and diagnostic agents.
27	www.allylix.com	6020 Cornerstone Court, Suite 260, San Diego, CA 92121	Allylix has developed proprietary technology that allows production of a group of natural products, called terpenes, at low cost.
28	www.alspinc.com	3030 Bunker Hill Street, Suite 104, San Diego, CA 92109	ALSP Inc. (American Life Science Pharmaceuticals, Inc.), is a privately held company, initially focused on developing new small molecule drugs for treating Alzheimer's disease.
29	www.alta-immunochem.com	3985 Sorrento Valley Blvd, San Diego, CA 92121	ALTA provides Liquid Chromatography Tandem Mass Spectrometry Services to pharmaceutical and chemical companies since its inception. The immunochemistry group has over 15 years of experience in the development of custom immunoassays.
30	www.altheadx.com	3550 Dunhill Street, San Diego, CA 92121	AltheaDx is bringing theranostics into clinical use and offers a wide range of molecular testing and assay development services using proprietary technology.
31	www.altheatech.com	11040 Roselle Street, San Diego, CA 92121-1205	Althea's services include high-throughput gene expression analysis using proprietary eXpress Profiling technology, custom real-time qPCR assay development services, cGMP protein and plasmid DNA production services.
32	www.altoris.com	11575 Sorrento Valley Road, San Diego, CA 92121-1321	Altoris provides tools that help the scientists in the modern drug discovery process, including intellectual property, discovery and optimization of drug candidates and lead targets.
33	www.ambitbio.com	4215 Sorrento Valley Blvd., San Diego, CA 92121	Ambit Biosciences is a privately-held biopharmaceutical company engaged in the discovery and development of small-molecule kinase inhibitors for the treatment of cancer.
34	www.ambrx.com	10975 North Torrey Pines Road, La Jolla, CA 92037	Ambrx is a leader in the field of protein optimization and developing protein/antibody drugs based on the site-specific incorporation of novel amino acids into proteins.
35	www.amchemicals.com	4065 Oceanside Blvd., Suite M, Oceanside,CA 92056-5824	AM Chemicals is a supplier of solid supports and reagents for oligonucleotide and organic synthesis on solid phase, and offers services in custom radiolabeling of synthetic oligonucleotides with 14C- and 3H-radionuclides.
36	www.amevolution.com	10300 Campus Pt Dr, Suite 200, San Diego 92121	AME is focused on applying its proprietary AMEsystem™ technology platform to the full range of protein therapeutic candidates including antibodies, cytokines, hormones and enzymes to develop novel human biotherapeutic candidates.
37	www.amirapharm.com	9535 Waples Street, Suite 100, San Diego, CA 92121	Amira Pharmaceuticals is a small molecule pharmaceutical company focused on the discovery and early development of compounds to treat inflammatory disease.

	COMPANY	ADDRESS	DESCRIPTION
38	www.amylin.com	9360 Towne Centre Drive, San Diego, California 92121	Amylin is focused on innovative therapies for people struggling with diabetes and obesity. SYMLIN is a synthetic version of the human hormone amylin and a diabetes therapy offering improved glucose control with potential for weight loss.
39	www.anaborex.com	2223 Avenida de la Playa #300, La Jolla, CA 92037	Anaborex is an early stage biotechnology company focused on metabolic disease.
40	www.anadyspharma.com	5871 Oberlin Drive, Suite 200, San Diego, CA 92121	Anadys Pharmaceuticals is a clinical-stage biopharmaceutical company focused on improving patient care by developing novel therapeutics for treatment of hepatitis C.
41	www.anaphoreinc.com	10931 North Torrey Pines Road, Suite 101, La Jolla, CA 92037	Anaphore unique protein engineering platform provides multiple approaches to generate Atrimer™ protein therapeutics with biological, manufacturing and commercial advantages over traditional drugs such as antibodies, proteins, and small molecules.
42	www.anaptysbio.com	10835 Road to the Cure, Suite 100, San Diego, CA 92121	AnaptysBio is a privately-held therapeutic antibody product company, focused on the application of somatic hypermutation for antibody discovery and optimization.
43	www.androscience.com	11175 Flintkote Ave., Suite. F, San Diego, CA 92121	AndroScience Corporation is a private biopharmaceutical company dedicated to the development and commercialization of a small molecule therapeutics, which target androgen-dependent diseases.
44	www.anticancer.com	7917 Ostrow St, San Diego, CA 92111	AntiCancer develops imaging technologies based on green fluorescent protein and related fluorescent proteins.
45	www.aquabounty.com	8375 Camino Santa Fe, San Diego, CA 92121	Aqua Bounty is developing advanced-hybrid salmon, trout, and tilapia designed to grow faster than traditional fish.
46	www.ardeabio.com	4939 Directors Place, San Diego, CA 92121	Ardea is a biotechnology company focused on the development of small-molecule therapeutics for the treatment of gout, cancer, inflammatory diseases and human immunodeficiency virus (HIV).
47	www.arenapharm.com	6154 Nancy Ridge Drive, San Diego, CA 92121	Arena is focused on the development of oral drugs for cardiovascular, central nervous system, inflammatory and metabolic diseases.
48	www.ariannecorp.com	9444 Waples Street, Suite 160, San Diego, CA 92121	Arianne offers scientific expertise in clinical and non-clinical development, US and International regulatory expertise, and clinical operations.
49	www.ari-inc.com	8989 Rio San Diego Drive, Suite 350, San Diego, CA 92108	Affiliated Research Institute (ARI) is an independent research facility conducting clinical medication studies for pharmaceutical companies.
50	www.arrayomics.com	9909 Hibert Street , Suite A, San Diego, CA 92131-1069	Arrayomics is developing a particle-based array technology, ArrayableESP, for multiplexed analysis.
51	www.aspire-irb.com	9320 Fuerte Dr., Suite 105, La Mesa, CA 91941	Aspire IRB operates in the field of ethical protection providing advanced human research protection.
52	www.atsbio.com	10451 Roselle Street, #300, San Diego, CA 92121	Advanced Targeting Systems is dedicated to providing targeting reagents for scientific research and pharmaceutical development, including targeted toxins, antibodies and custom services for the study of nervous system.

COMPANY	ADDRESS	DESCRIPTION
53 www.attenuon.com	11535 Sorrento Valley Road San Diego, CA 92121-1309	Attenuon develops a new generation of cancer therapeutics. The Company's drug candidates are designed to selectively disrupt multiple cellular processes important to tumor growth and metastasis.
54 www.atyrpharma.com	3565 General Atomics Court #103, San Diego CA 92121	aTyr Pharma is focused on identifying and developing of novel class of protein biologics to treat cancer, neurodegenerative diseases, inflammation, cardiovascular diseases and metabolic disorders.
55 www.auspexpharma.com	1261 Liberty Way, Suite C, Vista, CA 92081	Auspex is focused on the development of deuterated analogs of clinically validated drugs and applying this strategy to existing drugs for multiple therapeutic applications.
56 www.autogenomics.com	2251 Rutherford Road, Carlsbad, CA 92008	Autogenomics is focused on the development of automated microarray-based multiplexing molecular diagnostic platforms to assess disease signatures.
57 www.aviaradx.com	11025 Roselle Street, Suite 200, San Diego, CA 92121	bioTheranostics, part of the worldwide bioMérieux group, develops molecular diagnostic tests for support of individualized oncology therapies through improved cancer classification and better breast cancer prognosis.
58 www.avitacor.com	420 South Cedros, Solana Beach, CA 92075	Avitacor specializes in providing management, marketing, sales and scientific expertise of CRO services to pharmaceutical and biotechnology companies.
59 www.avivabio.com	11045 Roselle Street, #100, San Diego, CA 92121-1230	Aviva has pioneered cell-based platforms, leading to an innovative product (SealChip™), which has become the industry standard for ion channel-focused drug discovery.
60 www.avivasysbio.com	11025 Roselle Street, #100, San Diego, CA 92121	Aviva Systems Biology provides validated antibodies for study of biological systems and pathways, including antibodies to key targets in the areas of transcription, epigenetics and cell signaling.
61 www.b-alert.com	2237 Faraday Avenue, Suite 100, Carlsbad, CA 92008	Advanced Brain Monitoring is focused on neurocognitive profiling for personalized medicine, fatigue management, and the integration of neurophysiology into the human-computer interface.
62 www.behavioralpharma.com	665 San Rodolfo Drive, Suite 124, PMB 184 Solana Beach, CA 92075	Behavioral Pharma is a contract research organization delivering *in vivo* pre-clinical testing services applied to behavioral neuroscience research.
63 www.biocarta.com	3525 Del Mar Heights Rd., #244, San Diego, CA 92130 USA	BioCarta offers a forum for information exchange and collaboration between researchers, educators and students. The information falls into four categories: gene function, proteomic pathways, ePosters, and research reagents.
64 www.biocept.com	5810 Nancy Ridge Drive Suite 150, San Diego, CA 92121	Biocept is developing a new class of diagnostic assays for personalized medicine. The Cell Enrichment and Extraction platform captures target cells from heterogeneous cell population.
65 www.biocom.org	4510 Executive Drive, Plaza One, San Diego, CA 92121	Biocom is the largest regional life sciences association in the world representing more than 575 biotechnology, pharmaceutical and medical device/diagnostic companies throughout Southern California.

	COMPANY	ADDRESS	DESCRIPTION
66	www.bioformatix.com	12396 World Trade Drive, Suite 315, San Diego, CA 92128	BioFormatix is a research, product development, and service company focusing on the needs of biomedical markets. The Company's technology addresses data collection, data modeling, and software development.
67	www.biogenidec.com	5200 Research Place, San Diego, CA 92122	Biogen Idec is focused on the discovery, development, manufacturing, and commercialization of innovative therapies. Patients in more than 90 countries benefit from Biogen Idec's products that target diseases such as lymphoma, multiple sclerosis, and rheumatoid arthritis.
68	www.biolegend.com	11080 Roselle Street, San Diego, CA 92121	BioLegend develops and manufactures antibodies and reagents for biomedical research, product areas include cell immunophenotyping, cytokines and chemokines, adhesion, cancer research, T regulatory cells, stem cells, innate immunity, cell-cycle analysis, apoptosis, and modification-specific antibodies.
69	www.biomatrica.com	5627 Oberlin Drive, Suite 120, San Diego, CA 92121	Biomatrica is focused on the development of a novel technology, designed to prevent the degradation of complex biological samples during transport, storage and processing,
70	www.biomedicalstrategies.com	7729 Fay Avenue, La Jolla, CA 92037	BMS provides solutions to help clients maximize the profitibility of their medical products. The Company has experience in business & product development, market research, competitive analysis, product launches, government relations, scientific research, invention, and provides secure funding to emerging companies.
71	www.biomedica-usa.com	11622 El Camino Real, Suite 100, San Diego, CA 92130	BioMedica is a wholly owned subsidiary of Oxford Bio-Medica, a UK based biotechnology company specializing in the development of gene-based therapeutics for the treatment of cancer, neurodegenerative diseases and other disorders.
72	www.biomedicure.com	7940 Silverton Ave, Suite 107, San Diego, CA 92126, PO Box 261673	BioMedicure is a research-driven biopharmaceutical company dedicated to discovering and developing safe and effective products to prevent cancer, to kill meta-static cells, and to eliminate malignant solid tumors.
73	www.biomedirb.com	2525 Camino Del Rio South, Suite 300, San Diego, CA 92108	The Biomedical Research Institute of America is a non-profit independent Institutional Review Board dedicated to providing scholarships and programs for students to further their interest and education in science and research.
74	www.biomyx.net	10054 Mesa Ridge Court , Suite 112, San Diego, CA 92121	Biomyx offers a variety of services, including protein expression, signal transduction, protein labeling and mutagenesis. Biomyx also offers research tools such as D-siRNA.
75	www.bio-quant.com	6330 Nancy Ridge Drive, San Diego, CA 92121-3220	Bio-Quant is focused on providing biomedical services in the areas of pharmacology, pharmacokinetics and toxicology to support pre-IND studies and discovery programmes.

	COMPANY	ADDRESS	DESCRIPTION
76	www.biosite.com	9975 Summers Ridge Road, San Diego, CA 92121	Biosite has an expertise in rapid, high-capacity antibody development, enabling high throughput screening of diagnostic markers and cost-efficient development of high affinity antibodies for use in commercialized products.
77	www.biosurplus.com	10805 Vista Sorrento Parkway, Suite 200, San Diego, CA 92121	BioSurplus is a leading provider of pre-owned laboratory instruments and equipment management services.
78	www.biotheranostics.com	11025 Roselle Street, Suite 200, San Diego, CA 92121	bioTheranostics, part of the worldwide bioMérieux group, develops molecular diagnostic tests that support the selection of individualized oncology therapies through improved cancer classification.
79	www.biovascularinc.com	12230 El Camino Real, Suite 100, San Diego, California 92130	BioVascular is focused on developing saratin for either hemodialysis access grafts or peripheral bypass grafting until it is proven safe and effective in the clinic. The Company is developing a complementary platelet reduction product.
80	www.braincellsinc.com	3565 General Atomics Court, Suite 200, San Diego, CA 92121	BrainCells, a neurogenesis-based technology company, develops central nervous system medicines, including antidepressants for the treatment of depression and related mood disorders, with potential applications in cognition, post-traumatic stress disorder and brain repair.
81	www.brendan.com	2236 Rutherford Road, Suite 107, Carlsbad, California 92008	Brendan Technologies develops advanced commercial software to provide standardized software platform for all immunoassay and bioassay testing technologies.
82	www.burnham.org	10901 North Torrey Pines Road, La Jolla, CA 92037	Burnham Institute for Medical Research is dedicated to discovering the fundamental molecular causes of disease and devising the innovative therapies of tomorrow. The Institute is especially known for its world-class capabilities in stem cell research and drug discovery technologies.
83	www.bvsweb.com	2626 West Canyon Avenue, San Diego, CA 92123	BVS manages an evolving network of top-tier research and academic suppliers, delivering hundreds of vendor product shows, technical seminars and events across the US each year. BVS is a free service for biotech, pharmaceutical and academic research organizations.
84	www.cabrellis.com	9393 Towne Centre Drive, Suite 210, San Diego, CA 92121-3070	Cabrellis Pharmaceuticals is a new, specialty pharmaceutical company committed to the development of important therapies for the treatment of cancer. The Cabrellis development program centers on Calsed, a third generation synthetic anthracycline drug currently approved and commercialized for small-cell and non-small-cell lung cancers in Japan.
85	www.cadencepharm.com	12481 High Bluff Drive, Suite 200, San Diego, CA 92130	Cadence Pharmaceuticals focuses on the in-licensing, development, and commercialization of product candidates principally for use in the hospital setting in the United States and Europe.
86	www.calasiapharma.com	11494 Sorrento Valley Road, San Diego, CA	CalAsia Pharmaceuticals specializes in early stage drug discovery using structure-based drug design. The novel proprietary technology platform Differential Fragment-Based Screening is one of the most efficient approaches to discover and develop drug candidates.

	COMPANY	ADDRESS	DESCRIPTION
87	www.calcimedica.com	505 Coast Blvd South, Suite 209, La Jolla, CA 92037	CalciMedica is dedicated to the discovery and development of novel small molecule drugs for the treatment of autoimmune disorders, organ transplant rejection, and other immune diseases.
88	www.califiabio.com	11575 Sorrento Valley Road, Suite 217, San Diego, CA 92121	Califia Bio provides medicinal chemistry expertise, compound design, synthesis, pharmacokinetic optimization and drug discovery services in collaborations with NIH funded academic research groups and small biotech companies.
89	www.calmune.com	9393 Towne Centre Dr., Suite 130, San Diego, CA 92121	Calmune Corporation is a privately held biotechnology company developing antibody therapeutics for humans.
90	www.cassiallc.com	info@cassiallc.com	Cassia is a small biotechnology company that specializes in synthesis of isotopically labeled nucleotides for biomedical research.
91	www.cato.com	6480 Weathers Place, Suite 104, San Diego, CA 92121	Cato Research is designing and implementing nonclinical, regulatory, product development, manufacturing, and clinical strategies for drugs, biologics, and medical devices.
92	www.cellapplications.com	5820 Oberlin Drive, Suite 101, San Diego, CA92121	Cell Applications provides primary cell culture systems, including a wide array of primary cell types, optimized growth media, cell culture reagents, and antibodies.
93	www.celula-inc.com	7360 Carroll Road Suite 200 San Diego, CA 92121	Celula develops a microfluidics-based platform for cell-based assays and develops diagnostic systems for various medical treatments.
94	www.ceregene.com	9381 Judicial Drive, Suite 130, San Diego, CA 92121	Ceregene is focused on the treatment of major neurodegenerative disorders using the delivery of nervous system growth factors.
95	www.chembridge.com	16981 Via Tazon, Suite G, San Diego, CA 92127	ChemBridge Corporation offers an extensive portfolio of advanced discovery chemistry products and contract research services.
96	www.chemdiv.com	6605 Nancy Ridge Drive, San Diego, CA 92121	ChemDiv is a provider of integrated discovery and development solutions based on a chemistry platform. Integrated Discovery outSource™ covers the complete range of disciplines required to bring a project in CNS, oncology, inflammation, metabolic and infectious disease area from defining biological targets to identification of clinical drug candidates.
97	www.chimeros.com	3545 John Hopkins Ct, Suite 210, San Diego, CA 92121-1121	Chimeros is a cancer therapeutics company focused on the development of novel targeted treatments.
98	www.chinabiollc.com	3525 Del Mar Heights Rd, #463 San Diego, CA 92130	ChinaBio® LLC is connecting China biotech with the world. The Company provides a wide range of services to help entrepreneurs, investors, big pharma and biotech achieve success in China.
99	www.cibus.com	4025 Sorrento Valley Blvd., San Diego, CA 92121	Cibus, a trait development company, produces crop traits for the agricultural community.
100	www.clinicomp.com	9655 Towne Centre Drive, San Diego, CA 92121	A pioneer in its field, CliniComp develops advanced clinician documentation systems for hospitals, integrated delivery networks, academic medical centers and other acute care providers.

	COMPANY	ADDRESS	DESCRIPTION
101	www.clin-pharma.com	info@clin-pharma.com	ClinPharma Resources (ClinPharma Services, Inc.) offers clinical pharmacology, general clinical, and drug development consulting services for pharmaceutical and biotech companies of all sizes.
102	www.codatherapeutics.com	10505 Sorrento Valley Rd, Suite 395, San Diego, CA 92121	CoDa Therapeutics is focused on the development and commercialization of a new generation of wound care therapeutics known as "gap junction modulators."
103	www.comprendia.com		Comprendia is a consulting firm dedicated to the marketing and business development needs of small to mid-size biotechnology companies.
104	www.covx.com	9381 Judicial Drive, Suite 200, San Diego, CA 92121	CovX is a biotechnology company creating long-acting biotherapeutics. The CovX technology unites the therapeutic attractiveness of peptides with the beneficial properties of antibodies, resulting in a new biopharmaceutical, CovX-Body.
105	www.cpsonline.info	4311 Third Avenue, San Diego, CA 92103	San Diego Hospice and Palliative Care is international leader in "education and research in the art and science of palliative care."
106	www.cqihealthcare.com	2726 Shelter Island Drive, Suite 316, San Diego, CA 92106	CQI is an international healthcare management consulting firm that develops and implements regulatory and accreditation compliant, cost-effective Utilization, Quality, Case and Disease Management strategy and programs for healthcare and employer organizations.
107	www.csifinancial.com	3636 Nobel Drive, Suite 215, San Diego, CA 92122	CSI is a leader in patient loan programs and since inception has funded almost a quarter billion dollars in patient loans to hospitals and other types of healthcare providers located throughout the United States.
108	www.cylenepharma.com	5820 Nancy Ridge Drive, Suite 200, San Diego, CA 92121	Cylene Pharmaceuticals is a Phase II clinical-stage biotechnology company dedicated to the discovery, development and commercialization of targeted small-molecule drugs to treat life-threatening cancers.
109	www.cyntellect.com	6620 Mesa Ridge Road, San Diego, CA	Cyntellect is dedicated to setting new standards in cell analysis, purification, and processing technology. The technology utilizes *in situ*, microplate-based cytometry to analyze cells with minimal sample manipulation and to process cells with efficiency.
110	www.cypressbio.com	4350 Executive Drive, Suite 325, San Diego, CA 92121	Cypress Bioscience provides therapeutics and personalized medicine services to facilitate improved and individualized patient care.
111	www.cytoritx.com	3020 Callan Road, San Diego, CA 92121	Cytori pioneered the therapeutic use of a mixed or heterogenous population of uncultured cell types found in adipose tissue.
112	www.dartneuroscience.com	7473 Lusk Blvd., San Diego, CA 92121	Dart NeuroScience is focused on discovery of new technologies and therapeutics to help maximize cognitive vitality throughout life.
113	www.digirad.com	13950 Stowe Drive, Poway, CA 92064-8803	Digirad is a publicly-held company and a leading developer and manufacturer of solid-state gamma cameras for nuclear cardiology and general nuclear medicine applications.

	COMPANY	ADDRESS	DESCRIPTION
114	www.dow.com	5501 Oberlin Drive, San Diego, CA 92121	Dow delivers a broad range of products and services to customers in approximately 160 countries, connecting chemistry, innovation and sustainability.
115	www.ebdgroup.com	2032 Corte del Nogal, Suite 120, Carlsbad, CA 92011 USA	EBD Group is a leading partnering firm for the global life science industry, facilitating the biotech-pharma partnerships to deliver healthcare treatments to patients worldwide.
116	www.ebioscience.com	10255 Science Center Drive, San Diego, CA 92121	EBioscience develops and markets antibodies and research reagents to pharmaceutical, biotechnology, and medical research sectors. The company offers immuno-blotting detection reagents, cellular antigens, monoclonal and polyclonal antibodies, and cytokines.
117	www.eidogen.com	9381 Judicial Drive, Suite 200, San Diego, CA 92121	Eidogen-Sertanty is dedicated to delivering pioneering informatics technologies that will drive drug discovery in the post-genomic era.
118	www.epicept.com	6650 Nancy Ridge Drive, San Diego, CA 92121	EpiCept is focused on the development and commercial-ization of pharmaceutical products for the treatment of cancer and pain.
119	www.epitopediagnostics.com	8940 Activity Road, Suite G, San Diego, CA 92126	Epitope Diagnostics develops, manufactures and markets niche ELISA kits and innovative rapid tests for the world-wide diagnostic community.
120	www.eurogentec.com	11111 Flintkote Avenue, San Diego CA 92121-1222	Eurogentec is a provider of research, diagnostic and thera-peutic services with expertise in oligonucleotides, real-time qPCR, peptides, proteins, antibodies and arrays.
121	www.excaliard.com	2141 Palomar Airport Road, Suite 300, Carlsbad, CA92011	Excaliard has licensed a patented, clinically proven tech-nology with multiple therapeutic opportunities in fibrosis.
122	www.exelixis.com	4757 Nexus Centre Drive, San Diego, CA 92121	Exelixis targets multiple receptor tyrosine kinases simul-taneously, as well as components of key components of downstream signaling pathways that play important roles in cancer and metabolic diseases.
123	www.exonbio.com	6650 Lusk Blvd., Suite B108, San Digeo, CA 92121	Exon BioSystems has a proprietary GeneWizard gene synthesis and mammalian expression platforms for gene synthesis and recombinant protein production.
124	www.explorabiolabs.com	3030 Bunker Hill St., San Diego, CA 92109-5754	Explora BioLabs is a contract research organization that provides preclinical in vivo contract research and rental vivarium services.
125	www.eyecyte.com	3366 N. Torrey Pines Ct., Suite. 130, La Jolla, CA 92037	EyeCyte is dedicated to developing regenerative therapies for the treatment of ophthalmic diseases.
126	www.fallbrook-eng.com	355 West Grand Avenue, Suite 4, Escondido, CA 92025	Fallbrook Engineering is a contract product development, management, and engineering services consulting firm.
127	www.fatetherapeutics.com	10931 North Torrey Pines Rd, Suite 107, La Jolla, CA 92037	Fate Therapeutics is focused on the fundamental biologi-cal mechanisms that guide cell fate to develop stem cell therapeutics.
128	www.femtapharma.com	4510 Executive Drive, Suite 322, San Diego, CA 92121	Femta Pharmaceuticals is a private company, which is focused on development of protein therapeutics.

	COMPANY	ADDRESS	DESCRIPTION
129	www.ferringr.com	4245 Sorrento Valley Blvd., San Diego, CA 92121	Ferring Pharmaceuticals identifies, develops and markets innovative products in the fields of endocrinology, gastroenterology, infertility, obstetrics, urology and osteoarthritis.
130	www.genbio.com	15222 Avenue of Science, Suite A, San Diego, CA 92128	GenBio is a medical diagnostic company focused on infectious disease and autoimmune disease diagnostics.
131	www.gene.com	One Antibody Way, Oceanside, CA 92056-5701	Genentech is focused on discovery, development, manufacturing and commercialization of biotherapeutics that address significant medical needs.
132	www.genego.com	169 Saxony Road, #104, Encinitas, CA 92024	GeneGo is a provider of data mining and analysis solutions in systems biology for a wide range of applications in life science research and drug development.
133	www.genlantis.com	10190 Telesis Court, San Diego, CA 92121	Genlantis designs, develops and commercializes biological reagents for life sciences. The Company is focused on the development of protein expression tools and efficient molecule delivery.
134	www.genomatica.com	10520 Wateridge Circle, San Diego, CA 92121	Genomatica is a chemical company that commercializes bio-manufacturing processes for production of industrial chemicals.
135	www.genoptix.com	2110 Rutherford Road, Carlsbad, CA 92008	Genoptix is a specialized laboratory service provider focused on delivering personalized and comprehensive diagnostic services to hematologists and oncologists.
136	www.gen-probe.com	10210 Genetic Center Drive, San Diego, CA 92121	Gen-Probe is a leader in the development, manufacture and marketing of rapid, accurate and cost-effective nucleic acid tests for diagnosis of human diseases.
137	www.gentarget.com	9865 Mesa Rim Road, Suite 207, San Diego, CA 92121	GenTarget provides researchers with proprietary bioreagents and services in cell culture, living cell imaging, high thoughtput cloning and RNAi screening, and antibody engineering.
138	www.gentiva.com	2525 Camino Del Rio South Suite 220, San Diego, CA 92108-3719	Gentiva Health Services is the nation's leading provider of comprehensive home healthcare and related services, including disease and pain management.
139	www.genvault.com	6190 Corte Del Cedro, Carlsbad, CA 92011-1515	GenVault Corporation provides integrated archiving and retrieval solutions for organizations managing DNA collections.
140	www.genwaybio.com	6777 Nancy Ridge Drive, San Diego, CA 92121	GenWay develops and produces domain-specific IgY antibodies for immunoaffinity capture, partitioning, detection and analyses.
141	www.glloomis.com	990 Highland Drive, Suite 212Q, Solana Beach, CA 92075	G. L. Loomis & Associates provides personalized patent services to small companies, start-up enterprises, individual inventors and entrepreneurs.
142	www.glysens.com	6450 Lusk Boulevard, Suite E-109, San Diego, California 92121	GlySens is focused on developing a long term glucose sensor system to continuously monitor glucose levels and enhance the care and treatment of diabetes.
143	www.gnf.org	10675 John Jay Hopkins Drive, San Diego CA 92121	The Genomics Institute of the Novartis Research Foundation (GNF) is one of the Novartis international Corporate Research institutes.

COMPANY	ADDRESS	DESCRIPTION
144 www.governanceinstitute.com	6333 Greenwich Drive, Suite 200, San Diego, CA 92122	The Governance Institute is a membership organization serving not-for-profit hospital and health system boards of directors, executives, and physician leadership.
145 www.halozyme.com	11388 Sorrento Valley Road, San Diego, CA 92121	Halozyme is developing and commercializing products targeting the extracellular matrix for the drug delivery, oncology, and dermatology markets.
146 www.hbri.org	5310 Eastgate Mall, San Diego, CA 92121	The Human BioMolecular Research Institute (HBRI) is a non-profit research institute with focus on Alzheimer's disease and related neurodegenerative disorders, Parkinson's disease, depression, attention deficit disorder, drug abuse, pain and smoking cessation.
147 www.helicontherapeutics.com	7473 Lusk Blvd, Suite 100, San Diego, CA 92075	Helicon Therapeutics is focused on discovery of therapeutics to treat disorders of cognition through study of the genetic basis of long-term memory formation.
148 www.helixis.com	5421 Avenida Encinas, Suite B, Carlsbad, CA 92008	Helixis is a developer of advanced nucleic acid analysis tools that are based on novel technologies from the Caltech labs of Nobel Laureate David Baltimore and Axel Scherer.
149 www.hln.com	8449 Christopher Ridge Terrace, San Diego, CA 92127	NLH Consulting offers technology consulting services to public health agencies and their not-for-profit partners and facilitates the collaboration between health care and public health communities.
150 www.hlsresearch.com	3366 North Torrey Pines Court, Suite 310, La Jolla, CA 92037	HLS Research is an employee-owned company of scientists and engineers dedicated to basic and applied research in a variety of wave propagation phenomena, specializing in underwater acoustics.
151 www.holliseden.com	4435 Eastgate Mall, Suite 400, San Diego, CA 92121	Hollis-Eden Pharmaceuticals is the world leader in the development of a proprietary class of adrenal steroid hormones as novel pharmaceuticals for human health.
152 www.huyabio.com	12531 High Bluff Drive, Suite 138, San Diego, CA 92130	Huya Bioscience International is a leader in enabling and accelerating the global co-development of novel biopharmaceutical product opportunities originating in China.
153 www.ichorms.com	6310 Nancy Ridge Drive, Suite 107, San Diego, CA 92121	Ichor Medical Systems is focused on the development and commercialization of electroporation-mediated DNA drug products to treat or life threatening diseases.
154 biosystems.icxt.com	505 Coast Boulevard South, Suite 309, La Jolla, CA 92037	ICx Biosystems develops technologies for molecular diagnosis, focused on detection and identification of airborne threats; genomic methods for non-invasive prenatal diagnosis; and methods of analyzing the genomes of rare circulating cells.
155 www.idtdna.com	6868 Nancy Ridge Drive, San Diego, CA 92121	Integrated DNA Technologies is focused on custom oligonucleotides synthesis and a development of innovative new biotechnologies.

	COMPANY	ADDRESS	DESCRIPTION
156	www.igetherapeutics.com	6042 Cornerstone Ct. Suite E, San Diego, CA 92121	IGE Therapeutics is focused on innovative lineage-specific biomarkers in cell and gene therapy treatment for allergic inflammation and cancers.
157	www.illumina.com	9865 Towne Centre Drive, San Diego, CA 92121-1975	Illumina has developed a comprehensive line of products that address the experimentation scale and the functional analysis required to achieve the goals of molecular medicine.
158	www.inovadx.com	9900 Old Grove Road, San Diego, CA, 92131-1638	Inova is dedicated exclusively to autoimmune diagnostics.
159	www.inovio.com	11494 Sorrento Valley Road, San Diego, CA	Inovio Biomedical is focused on discovery, development, and delivery of a new generation of vaccines, called DNA vaccines, to prevent or treat cancers and chronic infectious diseases.
160	www.internationalstemcell.com	2595 Jason Court , Oceanside, CA 92056	International Stem Cell Corporation is focused on the development of human stem cell lines that allow to eliminate the rejection of transplanted cells by the patient's immune system.
161	www.intrinsiclifesciences.com	505 Coast Boulevard South, Suite 102, La Jolla, CA 92037	Intrinsic LifeSciences performs the world's first human hepcidin ELISA test (hormone regulating iron homeostasis in humans) for leading pharmaceutical companies and clinical investigators worldwide.
162	www.invitrogen.com	5791 Van Allen Way PO Box 6482 Carlsbad, California 92008	Invitrogen is a global biotechnology tools company providing premier systems, consumables, and services for scientific researchers.
163	www.invivogen.com	3950 Sorrento Valley Blvd, Suite 100, San Diego, California 92121, USA	InvivoGen provides reagents for studying innate immunity including new products for research of inflammasomes. InvivoGen provides high-quality antibiotics and plasmids.
164	www.invivoscribe.com	6330 Nancy Ridge Drive, Suite 106, San Diego, CA 92121	InVivoScribe Technologies offers tools for molecular diagnostics, hematopathology and cDNA synthesis.
165	www.ionian-tech.com	4940 Carroll Canyon Road Suite #100, San Diego, CA 92121-1735	Ionian Technologies develops molecular diagnostics technology of the early detection of emerging and infectious diseases.
166	www.irisys.com	8810 Rehco Road, Suite F, San Diego, CA 92121	IriSys provides pharmaceutical product development contract services specializing in formulation development, tablet formulation, cGMP manufacturing of clinical trial materials, and consulting related to the drug development process.
167	www.isispharm.com	1896 Rutherford Road, Carlsbad, CA 92008-7326	Isis Pharmaceuticals develops RNA-based technologies and drug discovery platform based on antisense technology.
168	www.jadenbio.com	11575 Sorrento Valley Road, Suite 206, San Diego, CA 92121	Jaden BioScience specializes in developing and commercializing novel chemiluminescent research diagnostic assays for the scientific and medical communities.
169	www.janushealth.com	5030 Camino de la Siesta, Suite 405, San Diego, CA 92108	Janus Health develops innovative and patented mobile technologies that allow housecall physicians to bring an excellent level of health care to the home.

	COMPANY	ADDRESS	DESCRIPTION
170	www.jcvi.org	10355 Science Center Drive San Diego, CA 92121	The J. Craig Venter Institute is a pioneer in genomic research by using new computing and computational tools, as well as new DNA sequencing technology.
171	www.kalypsys.com	10420 Wateridge Circle, San Diego, CA 92121	Kalypsys is innovator in the area of drug discovery. Kalypsys has developed epiK™ – a proprietary and highly automated small molecule drug discovery platform.
172	www.kelaroo.com	4225 Executive Square, Suite 250, La Jolla, CA 92037	Kelaroo provides software solutions for the drug discovery and development companies. The company offers various services that range from drug discovery to commercial software development, database and IT administration, as well as project management services.
173	www.kentbioenergy.com	11125 Flintkote Avenue, San Diego, CA 92121	Kent BioEnergy employs commercially viable microalgae-based technologies for liquid fuel production, water pollution remediation, CO_2 capture, landfill management, and production of livestock feed additives.
174	www.kfxmed.com	5845 Avenida Encinas, Suite 128, Carlsbad, CA 92008-4432	KFx Medical is an innovator in proprietary implant systems that facilitate reattachment of soft tissue to bone in a variety of orthopedic sports medicine procedures.
175	www.kgi.edu	535 Watson Drive, Claremont, CA 91711	Keck Graduate Institute is focused on education and research in life sciences, aimed at translating into practice for the benefit of society.
176	www.kinexisinc.com	P.O. Box 130836, Carlsbad, CA 92013	Kinexis is a life science R&D company targeting soluble oligomeric conformations of pathologic amyloid proteins involved in multiple neurodegenerative and non-CNS diseases.
177	www.krm-associates.com	11956 Bernardo plaza Dr, Suite 417, San Diego, CA 92128	KRM Associates is a regulatory due diligence advisory practice for the health care industry specialized in domestic and international regulatory requirements for a wide variety of medical products.
178	kyowa-kirin-ca.com	9420 Athena Circle, La Jolla, CA 92037	Kyowa Hakko Kirin California is focused on developing fully human antibody based therapeutics in four major disease areas: oncology, renal diseases, immune disorders and allergy.
179	www.liai.org	9420 Athena Circle, La Jolla, CA 92037	La Jolla Institute for Allergy and Immunology is focused on understanding the immune response to infectious agents and cancers and the prevention, treatment and cure of immune system diseases.
180	www.lifetechnologies.com	5791 Van Allen Way, Carlsbad, CA 92008	Life Technologies is a global biotechnology tools company dedicated to improving the human condition.
181	www.ligand.com	10275 Science Center Drive, San Diego, CA 92121	Ligand's programs span in large market indications, such as muscle wasting, frailty, hormone-related diseases, osteoporosis, inflammatory diseases, anemia, asthma, rheumatoid arthritis and psoriasis.

	COMPANY	ADDRESS	DESCRIPTION
182	www.lithera.com	9191 Towne Center Drive, Suite 400, San Diego, CA 92122	Lithera develops products for esthetic medicine to enhance wellbeing and improve quality of life.
183	www.ljbi.org	505 Coast Boulevard South, Suite 406, La Jolla, CA 92037	The focus of the Institute's research is to determine how mechanical forces play a role in the normal physiology and pathology of blood vessels, bone, and muscle.
184	www.ljpc.com	4365 Executive Drive, Suite 300, San Diego, California, 92121-2125	La Jolla Pharmaceutical Company is focused on the development and testing of Riquent® (abetimus sodium), as a treatment for patients with lupus.
185	www.lmana.com	4660 La Jolla Village Drive, Suite 900, San Diego, CA 92122	LMA designs, develops, markets and distributes medical equipment, principally the LMA™ laryngeal mask airway line of supraglottic airway device products.
186	www.lpath.com	6335 Ferris Square, Suite A, San Diego, CA 92121	Lpath is a leader in lipid-based therapeutics, a field of medical science whereby bioactive signaling lipids are targeted for treating human diseases.
187	www.luminousmedical.com	1920 Palomar Point Way, Carlsbad, CA 92008	Luminous Medical provides automated glucose management systems that empower health care professionals to improve outcomes of critically ill patients.
188	www.mabvax.com	11588 Sorrento Valley Rd., Suite 20, San Diego, CA 92121	MabVax Therapeutics is focused on developing and commercializing novel vaccines and human antibodies for the treatment of cancer.
189	www.mandalabio.com	6755 Mira Mesa Blvd, Suite 123-187, San Diego, CA 92121	Mandala Biosciences is focusing on providing new tools and technologies to the stem cell research community.
190	www.mappbio.com	6160 Lusk Blvd. # C105 San Diego, CA 92121	Mapp Biopharmaceutical develops novel pharmaceuticals for the prevention and treatment of infectious diseases, focusing on global health and biodefense.
191	www.mbasis.com	11119 North Torrey Pines Road, La Jolla, CA 92037	Metabasis is focused on the discovery, development and commercialization of novel drugs by applying its proprietary technologies for targeting the liver and liver pathways.
192	www.mbpinc.com	9389 Waples Street, San Diego, CA 92121-3903	MBP is provider of disposable lab supplies to the life science industry. The Company delivers a broad selection of analytical instruments, equipment, consumables and laboratory supplies.
193	www.medicinova.com	4350 La Jolla Village Drive, Suite 950, San Diego, CA 92122	MediciNova is focused on development of small molecule therapeutics for diseases including multiple sclerosis, asthma, interstitial cystitis, solid tumor cancers, and generalized anxiety disorder.
194	www.medigene.com	10650 Scripps Ranch Blvd. Suite 230, San Diego, CA 92131	MediGene concentrates on researching, developing, and commercializing novel drugs for cancer and autoimmune diseases.
195	www.medisteminc.com	9255 Towne Centre Drive, Suite 450, San Diego, CA 92122	Medistem is focused on development and commercialization of technologies related to adult stem cell extraction and manipulation for use in treating inflammatory and degenerative diseases.
196	www.medivas.com	6275 Nancy Ridge Drive, San Diego, CA 92121	MediVas has developed a unique platform of biocompatible, biodegradable synthetic polymers for injection or implantation as drug delivery or tissue regeneration materials.

COMPANY	ADDRESS	DESCRIPTION
197 www.mednovus.com	664 Hymettus Avenue, Leucadia, CA 92024 USA	Mednovus is focused on providing advanced and sensible ferromagnetic detection technologies.
198 www.microconstants.com	9050 Camino Santa Fe, San Diego, CA 92121	MicroConstants is a Contract Research Organization providing high quality, efficient bioanalytical, drug metabolism and pharmacokinetic support to the biotech industry.
199 www.microislet.com	6370 Nancy Ridge Drive, Suite 112, San Diego, CA 92121	MicroIslet is engaged in the research, development, and commercialization of patented technologies in the field of transplantation therapy for people with insulin-dependent diabetes.
200 www.milleniumlaboratories.com	16981 Via Tazon, Suite F, San Diego, CA 92127	Millennium Laboratories is focused on the treatment of chronic pain. The Company's products provide the fastest turn-around time in the industry for drug test reporting and confirmation of results.
201 www.millennium.com	10975 Torreyana Road, San Diego, CA 92121	Millennium is focused on the development of cancer therapeutics. The Company develops and markets VELCADE for the treatment of patients with multiple myeloma and relapsed mantle cell lymphoma.
202 www.minnowmedical.com	10911 Technology Drive, San Diego, California 92127	Minnow Medical has developed an innovative endovascular Guided Reshaping Technology™ (GRT™) for effective treatment of peripheral arterial disease
203 www.mixturesciences.com	3550 General Atomics Ct., San Diego, CA 92121	Mixture Sciences specializes in biomedical research and drug discovery for the treatment of HIV/AIDS, cancer, diabetes, multiple sclerosis, and infectious diseases, including Lyme Disease.
204 www.mobio.com	2746 Loker Avenue West, Carlsbad, CA 92010	MO BIO Laboratories offers a line of nucleic acid purification kits. MO BIO's Power® kits contain patented Inhibitor Removal Technology™.
205 www.molecularthroughput.com	1425 Russ Blvd. T107D, San Diego, CA 92101	Molecular Throughput is a contract research organization that specializes in custom recombinant protein production for pharmaceutical and biotechnology research companies.
206 www.molsoft.com	3366 North Torrey Pines Court, Suite 300, La Jolla, CA 92037	Molsoft a leading provider of tools, databases and consulting services in the area of structure prediction, structural proteomics, bioinformatics, cheminformatics, molecular visualization and animation, and rational drug design.
207 www.mpexpharma.com	11535 Sorrento Valley Road, San Diego, CA 92121	Mpex Pharmaceuticals develops new therapies to combat the growing issue of antibiotic resistance, with a particular focus on gram-negative organisms.
208 www.multigen-diagnostics.com	11568 Sorrento Valley Road, Suite 8, San Diego, CA 92121	MultiGEN Diagnostics is a source for infectious disease diagnosis, genetic susceptibility to disease, mutation based therapeutic decisions.
209 www.nanogen.com	10398 Pacific Center Court, San Diego, CA 92121	Nanogen products include molecular diagnostic kits and reagents, and rapid test kits, which can be used in urgent care settings or at the point-of-care.
210 www.nanoimagingservices.com	10931 N Torrey Pines Rd., Suite 108, San Diego, CA 92037	NanoImaging Services provides nanoparticle characterization services for use in early and late stage drug development processes.

	COMPANY	ADDRESS	DESCRIPTION
211	www.nanosyn.com	11558 Sorrento Valley Road, San Diego, California 92121	Nanosyn, provider of Chemistry on Demand services, is a medicinal chemistry based organization providing innovative solutions for drug discovery.
212	www.natural-selection.com	9330 Scranton Road, Suite 150, San Diego, CA 92121	Natural Selection has developed a suite of computational tools for small molecule lead discovery and optimization.
213	www.ndtcorp.com	501 Via Del Monte, Oceanside, CA 92058	NDT offers a unique solution to *in vivo* siRNA delivery by designing novel biodegradable delivery vehicles with the combined ability to target specific cells and efficiently deliver the therapeutic moiety to the target cells.
214	www.neomps.com	9395 Cabot Drive, San Diego, CA 92126	NeoMPS is an expert in peptide production.
215	www.nereuspharm.com	10480 Wateridge Circle, San Diego, CA 92121	Nereus Pharmaceuticals is a pioneer in the discovery and development of new therapeutics for cancer, inflammatory and infectious diseases that were derived from marine microbial sources.
216	www.neurocrine.com	12780 El Camino Real, San Diego, CA 92130	Neurocrine Biosciences is a product based biopharmaceutical company focusing on the development and commercialization of innovative pharmaceutical products.
217	www.nexbio.com	10665 Sorrento Valley Road, San Diego, CA 92121	NexBio focus is drug development for prevention and treatment of human respiratory viral infections such as influenza.
218	www.nexusbio.com	12140 Community Road, Poway, CA 92064 USA	Nexus Biosystems engages in the development and provision of technologies and automation systems for pharmaceutical, biotech, agrochemical, and academic research centers worldwide.
219	www.novabiotech.com	1906 Grove Road, El Cajon, CA 92020	Nova Biotech provides service and sales support for Uv/Vis Spectrophotometers, Spectrofluorometers, Microplate Readers, FTIR, PCR, HPLC, FPLC and Temperature Control instruments.
220	www.novalar.com	12555 High Bluff Drive, Suite 300, San Diego, CA 92130	Novalar is a privately-held specialty pharmaceutical company focused on bringing novel solutions to dentistry.
221	www.novarx.com	6828 Nancy Ridge Drive, Suite 100, San Diego, CA 92121	NovaRx Corporation is a clinical-stage biopharmaceutical company dedicated to the development and commercialization of novel cell-based therapeutic vaccines for cancer treatment.
222	www.novelix.com	8008 Girard Ave, Suite 330, La Jolla, CA 92037	Novelix Pharmaceuticals is committed to developing innovative, proprietary, dermatology products with large market potential to treat skin diseases.
223	www.novocell.com	3550 General Atomics Court, San Diego, CA 92121	Novocell is a stem cell engineering company dedicated to creating, delivering and commercializing cell and drug therapies to treat diabetes and other chronic diseases.
224	www.nuvasive.com	7475 Lusk Blvd., San Diego, CA 92121 USA	NuVasive is a medical device company focused on the design, development, and marketing of products for the surgical treatment of spine disorders.
225	www.oceratherapeutics.com	12651 High Bluff Drive, Suite 230, San Diego, CA, 92130	Ocera Therapeutics develops and commercializes therapeutics for gastrointestinal and liver diseases.

	COMPANY	ADDRESS	DESCRIPTION
226	www.optimerpharma.com	10110 Sorrento Valley Rd., Suite C, San Diego, CA 92121	Optimer is focused on discovering, developing, and commercializing innovative anti-infective products in diseases of unmet needs.
227	www.orbigen.com	6827 Nancy Ridge Drive, San Diego, CA 92121	Orbigen develops, manufactures and markets reagent tools for proteomic research. The Company is best known for novel antibodies, innovative gene expression technologies, and reliable custom protein expression services.
228	www.orexigen.com	3344 N. Torrey Pines Court, Suite 200, La Jolla CA, CA 92037	Orexigen Therapeutics is focused on the development of pharmaceutical product candidates for the treatment of obesity.
229	www.orphagen.com	11494 Sorrento Valley, San Diego, CA 92121	Orphagen Pharmaceuticals is focused on major unmet medical needs by developing innovative small molecule drugs targeting orphan nuclear receptors.
230	www.otonomy.com	5626 Oberlin Drive, Suite 100, San Diego, CA 92121	Otonomy is focused on the development and commercialization of novel treatments for diseases of the ear.
231	www.paceturf.org	1267 Diamond St., San Diego, CA 92109	The PACE Turf information service delivers science-based solutions to turf management problems with research news, information and expert advice.
232	www.pacificgmp.com	8810 Rehco Road, Suite E, San Diego, CA 92121	PacificGMP is a contract manufacturer in utilizing bioprocessing for cGMP and non-GMP services ranging from cell line optimization, early process design, development and scale-up, to preclinical and clinical biologics manufacturing, purification and fill/finish.
233	www.pacificsleepmedicine.com	10052 Mesa Ridge Court, Suite 101, San Diego, CA 92121	Pacific Sleep Medicine Services provides individual consultations and diagnostic evaluations for patients who suffer from sleep disorders.
234	www.pacificworlddiscovery.com	3550 General Atomics Ct, Building 9-202, San Diego, CA 92121	Pacific World Discovery is an outsourcing laboratory and chemistry services provider.
235	www.pacira.com	10450 Science Center Drive, San Diego, CA 92121	Pacira Pharmaceuticals is an acute care specialty pharmaceutical company dedicated to address the needs of the acute care market.
236	www.paramountbio.com	4365 Executive Drive, Suite 1500, San Diego, CA. 92121	Paramount BioSciences is a venture capital firm specializing in seed stage investments. The firm invests in new biotechnology, pharmaceutical, healthcare, and life-sciences companies.
237	www.pathway.com	4045 Sorrento Valley Blvd., San Diego, CA 92121	Pathway Genomics offers secure, comprehensive and affordable personal genomic information with ancestry and health tests. The Company provides the only DNA testing service with an on-site federal and state CLIA-licensed laboratory.
238	www.paxvax.com	3985A Sorrento Valley Blvd., San Diego, CA 92121	PaxVax is focused on developing candidate oral preventative vaccines against infectious diseases, such as influenza, cholera, anthrax, malaria and HPV.
239	www.perceptaassociates.com	7040 Avenida Encinas, Suite 104-365 Carlsbad CA 92011	Percepta specializes in life science marketing, strategic business planning, portfolio management, branding, and marketing communications.

	COMPANY	ADDRESS	DESCRIPTION
240	www.phamatech.com	10151 Barnes Canyon Road, San Diego, CA 92121	Phamatech is a health care company devoted to medical diagnostic, including discovery, development, and manufacture of diagnostic devices.
241	www.pharmatek.com	7330 Carroll Road, Suite 200, San Diego, CA 92121	Pharmatek is a pharmaceutical chemistry development organization supporting the pharmaceutical and biotechnology industries, assisting the client in bringing compounds from discovery to the clinic.
242	www.phenomixcorp.com	5930 Cornerstone Court West, Suite 230, San Diego, CA 92121	Phenomix is focused on the discovery, development and commercialization of novel small-molecules such as dutogliptin tartrate, a DPP-4 inhibitor for treatment for Type 2 diabetes.
243	www.philometron.com	10451 Roselle Street, Suite 100, San Diego, CA 92121	PhiloMetron™ is a healthcare company developing proprietary diagnostic products and services, focused on improving the quality and lowering the cost of health management.
244	www.photonicsresearchcorp.com	1493 Anchor Place, San Marcos, CA 92078	Photonics Research Corporation is a photonics technology consulting firm.
245	www.photothera.com	5925 Priestly Dr. Suite 120, Carlsbad, CA 92008	PhotoThera is a medical device company, developing proprietary, noninvasive laser energy therapies for clinical care and management of ischemic stroke, traumatic brain injury, global ischemia and disturbances in cellular metabolic function.
246	www.polypeptide.com	9395 Cabot Drive, San Diego, CA 92126	PolyPeptide Group offer expertise in peptide chemistry, customer-dedicated project teams, full FDA- and EMEA- conforming cGMP compliance.
247	www.ppti.com	10655 Sorrento Valley Road, San Diego, CA 92121	Protein Polymer Technologies is focused on development of products that aid in the natural process of bodily repair and tissue healing.
248	www.predictivebio.com	2120 Las Palmas Drive, Suite F, Carlsbad, CA 92011	Predictive Biology uses embryonic stem cells to accelerate drug discovery and develop innovative technologies for personalized medicine.
249	www.premierinc.com	12255 El Camino Real Suite 100, San Diego, CA 92130	Premier is focused on improving healthcare by collecting and analyzing clinical and financial data from its hospitals, organizing committees to make decisions and set direction for the alliance, sponsoring seminars and conferences, and sharing best practices.
250	www.proacta.com	9255 Towne Centre Drive, Suite 520, San Diego 92121	Proacta is a clinical-stage biopharmaceutical company working to develop hypoxia-activated prodrugs for the treatment of cancer.
251	www.proactatherapeutics.com	9255 Towne Centre Drive, Suite 520, San Diego 92121	Proacta's lead drug candidate is a small-molecule prodrug designed to improve the outcomes of patients with cancer by targeting cells that are resistant to chemotherapy and radiotherapy.
252	www.profil-research.com	855 3rd Avenue, Suite 4400, Chula Vista, CA 91911	Profil is a privately owned institute providing high quality early phase clinical research services in diabetes and obesity.

COMPANY	ADDRESS	DESCRIPTION
253 www.prometheuslabs.com	9410 Carroll Park Drive, San Diego, CA 92121	Prometheus is focused on delivery of diagnostic and therapeutic products for treatment of a wide variety of human diseases.
254 www.prosci-inc.com	12170 Flint Place, Poway, CA 92064	ProSci is an antibody supplier.
255 www.puracyp.com	5900 Sea Lion Place Suite 130, Carlsbad, CA 92010	Puracyp is focused on the development of methods that allow rapid and efficient assessment of the safety of drugs prior to their clinical usage.
256 www.purebio.com	1725 Gillespie Way, El Cajon, CA 92020	PURE Bioscience develops and markets bioscience safety products including silver dihydrogen citrate-based antimicrobials and boric acid-based pesticides.
257 www.qedbio.com	10919 Technology Place, Suite C, San Diego, CA 92127-1882	QED Bioscience develops novel monoclonal and poly-clonal antibody products for academic, biotechnology, diagnostic and pharmaceutical research clients.
258 www.quidel.com	10165 McKellar Court San Diego, CA 92121 USA	Quidel Corporation is developing, manufacturing and marketing rapid diagnostic solutions at the point-of-care in infectious diseases and reproductive health.
259 www.receptortech.com	9381 Judicial Drive, Suite 140, San Diego, CA 92121	Membrane Receptor Technologies applies NMR spectroscopy to examine interactions between drugs and membrane-associated receptors.
260 www.receptos.com	10835 Road to the Cure, Suite 205, San Diego, CA 92121	Receptos utilizes pioneering G-protein coupled receptos technology to facilitate structure-based drug design for drug development.
261 www.regenemed.com	9855 Towne Centre Drive, Suite 200, San Diego, CA 92121	RegeneMed is focused on development of safer and effective drugs by providing integrated high through-put platforms and applying engineered human tissue-based assays.
262 www.regulusrx.com	1896 Rutherford Road, Carlsbad, CA, 92008-7208	Regulus Therapeutics is focused on discovery, development and commercialization of micro RNA-targeted therapeutics.
263 www.resmed.com	9001 Spectrum Center Blvd., San Diego, CA 92123	ResMed develops, manufactures and markets medical products for the treatment of respiratory disorders, with a focus on sleep-disordered breathing.
264 www.resolutions-llc.com	462 Stevens Ave, Suite 109, Solana Beach, CA 92075	RESolutions is focused on providing cost-effective, proven patient recruitment programs to biotech/pharmaceutical, medical device companies and Contract Research Organizations.
265 www.restech-corp.com	10804 Willow Ct., Suite B, San Diego, CA 92127	Restech is dedicated to providing comfortable, reliable solutions to assist physicians in the diagnosis of reflux related health problems.
266 www.retrogen.com	6645 Nancy Ridge Drive, San Diego, CA 92121	Retrogen is a provider of genomic products and services, including DNA sequencing, gene synthesis, siRNA, SNP discovery, mutagenesis, oligo synthesis, nucleic acid purification.
267 www.retrovirox.com	6605 Nancy Ridge Drive, San Diego, CA 92121	RetroVirox is dedicated to the discovery of new treatments for patients with infectious diseases, including HIV, HCV, and other serious infections.

	COMPANY	ADDRESS	DESCRIPTION
268	www.ribomed.com	1989 Palomar Oaks Way, Suite B, Carlsbad, CA 92011	RiboMed is focused on technology development for sensitive and specific DNA methylation profiling.
269	www.rmgmed.com	2466 First Avenue, Suite B, San Diego, CA 92101-1408	Radiation Medical Group assists with every aspect of cancer care, including prevention, diagnosis, treatment and recovery.
270	www.sagientresearch.com	3655 Nobel Drive Suite 540, San Diego, CA 92122	Sagient Research Systems develops, produces, and sells proprietary research products to mutual funds, hedge funds, and investment banks.
271	www.sandiegoimaging.com	7910 Frost Street, Suite 100, San Diego, CA 92123	San Diego Imaging Medical Group offers diagnostic imaging services.
272	www.sangart.com	6175 Lusk Blvd San Diego, CA 92121	Sangart is focused on developing and commercializing of life-saving medicines utilizing targeted oxygen delivery.
273	www.santarus.com	3721 Valley Centre Drive, 4th Floor, San Diego, CA 92130	Santarus is focused on acquisition, development, and commercialization of proprietary products and therapies that treat gastrointestinal diseases and disorders, including gastroesophageal reflux disease.
274	www.scantibodies.com	9336 Abraham Way, Santee, CA 92071 USA	Scantibodies Laboratory provides sensitive and accurate diagnostic tests.
275	www.sciencemedia.com	6450 Lusk Blvd, Suite E206, San Diego, CA 92121	ScienceMedia has established unique marketing and eLearning solutions for life sciences by integrating science expertise, molecular simulation, and web programming.
276	www.scripps.org	4275 Campus Point Ct., San Diego, CA 92121	Scripps Health is a nonprofit, community-based health care network.
277	www.sdcardiac.com	3131 Berger Avenue, Suite 200, San Diego, CA 92123	San Diego Cardiac Center is focused on patient education and providing life-enhancing treatments by dedicated cardiac specialists.
278	www.sdchp.com	3020 Children's Way, MC 5054, San Diego, CA 92123	The Center for Human Performance is a motion analysis organization associated with sports science, gait analysis, biomechanics, orthopedics, and motion capture for animation.
279	www.sdgkc.com	9834 Genesee Avenue, Suite 110, La Jolla, California 92037	San Diego Gamma Knife Center treats patients with brain tumors, AVMs, acoustic neuromas, essential tremors, trigeminal neuralgia and many other brain disorders.
280	www.sdhospice.com	4311 Third Avenue, San Diego, CA 92103, or 404 Camino Del Rio South, Suite 200, San Diego, CA 92108	San Diego Hospice and The Institute for Palliative Medicine are committed to promote quality of life at every stage of life, through patient and family care, education, research and advocacy.
281	www.selectivegenetics.com	11545 Sorrento Valley Road, Suite 310, San Diego, CA 92121	Selective Genetics technology platforms allow achievement of more efficient gene transfer and expression at the site of tissue repair than other forms of gene transfer.
282	www.senomyx.com	4767 Nexus Centre Drive, San Diego, California 92121	Senomyx is using proprietary technologies to discover and develop flavors, flavor enhancers and bitter blockers for the food, beverage, and ingredient supply industries.
283	www.sequelpharma.com	12750 High Bluff Drive, Suite 300, San Diego, CA 92130	Sequel Pharmaceuticals is focused on cardiovascular drug development.

	COMPANY	ADDRESS	DESCRIPTION
284	www.sequenom.com	3595 John Hopkins Court, San Diego, CA 92121-1331	Sequenom is providing solutions for biomedical research, agricultural applications, molecular medicine and noninvasive prenatal diagnostics research.
285	www.shrinknano.com	2038 Corte Del Nogal, Suite 110, Carlsbad, California 92011	Shrink Nanotechnologies is focused on innovative nano-fabrication platform, which provides for the rapid design and low-cost fabrication of micro and nanostructures for devices with a wide range of applications.
286	www.skinsurgerymed.com	5222 Balboa Avenue 5th & 6th Floor, San Diego, CA 92117	Skin Surgery Medical Group are contracted by pharmaceutical companies to participate in Phase I, II, III, and IV clinical trials for FDA approval on medications and devices.
287	www.solulink.com	9853 Pacific Heights Blvd. Suite H, San Diego, CA 92121	SoluLinK is focused on development of products for conjugation of biomolecules.
288	www.somaxon.com	3830 Valley Centre Drive, Suite 705-461, San Diego, CA 92130-3323	Somaxon Pharmaceuticals is focused on licensing, development and commercialization of products for the treatment of diseases of the central nervous system.
289	www.spectral-imaging.com	1497 Poinsettia Avenue, Suite 158, Vista, CA 92081	Applied Spectral Imaging develops and manufactures comprehensive solutions for cytogenetics and pathology imaging and data management needs.
290	www.srisd.com	826 Orange Avenue, Suite 633, Coronado, CA 92118	Spine Research Institute of San Diego (SRISD) is focused on whiplash and brain injury traumatology.
291	www.stemagen.com	4150 Regents Park Row, Suite 275, La Jolla, CA 92037	Stemagen is focused on embryonic stem cell research.
292	www.stemedica.com	5375 Mira Sorrento Pl, Suite 100, San Diego, CA 92121	Stemedica Cell Technologies develops adult stem cell lines.
293	www.stemgent.com	10575 Roselle Street, San Diego, CA 92121 USA	Stemgent is a stem cell reagent company.
294	www.stratagene.com	11011 N. Torrey Pines Road, La Jolla, CA 92037	Stratagene develops, manufactures, and markets life science research and diagnostic products.
295	www.stratbiocat.com	10420 Wateridge Circle, Suite 100, San Diego, CA 92121	Strategic Enzyme Applications (SEA) develops low cost applications for chemical manufacture and specializes in application of biocatalysis for the design, development and implementation of pioneering process chemistries.
296	www.strubix.com	10929 Technology Place, San Diego CA 92127	Structural Bioinformatics (SBI) is focused on proteomics-driven drug discovery and use of protein structural information to accelerate the discovery and optimization processes.
297	www.synteract.com	5759 Fleet Street, Suite 100, Carlsbad, CA 92008	Synteractis is focused on clinical research, technology, and safety needs with emphasis in oncology, central nervous system, cardiovascular disease, and ophthalmology.
298	www.syntheticgenomics.com	11149 North Torrey Pines Road, La Jolla, CA 92037	Synthetic Genomics is developing genomic-driven commercial solutions for production of clean fuels and biochemicals.

	COMPANY	ADDRESS	DESCRIPTION
299	www.takedasd.com	10410 Science Center Drive, San Diego, CA 92121	Takeda San Diego (TSD) is Takeda's center for excellence in structure-based drug discovery. TSD is focused on protein crystallography and drug discovery technologies to cure metabolic diseases and cancer.
300	www.targegen.com	9380 Judicial Drive, San Diego, CA 92121	TargeGen develops small molecule kinase inhibitors for the treatment of hematological malignancies and other disorders.
301	www.teamreva.com	5751 Copley Drive, Suite B, San Diego, CA 92111	REVA Medical is develops minimally invasive bioresorbable coronary medical devices.
302	www.theaequitasgroup.com	12680 High Bluff Drive, Suite 110 , San Diego, California 92130	The Aequitas Group is a healthcare advisory firm that specializes in developing clinical and economic solutions that define product values.
303	www.thebindingsite.com	5889 Oberlin Drive Suite 101 San Diego CA 92121	Binding Site is focused on research, development and manufacture of immunodiagnostic assays in the fields of B cell disorders and investigation of the immune response.
304	www.thenicholasconorinstitute.org	9710 Scranton Road, Suite 170 San Diego, California 9212	The Nicholas Conor Institute is focused on identifying and developing both innovative therapies and original diagnostic approaches to treating childhood cancer.
305	www.therakem.com	2260 El Cajon Blvd., Suite 183, San Diego, CA 92104	TheraKem has developed methods for preparation of novel fluorinated compounds and chiral alpha-substituted-beta-amino acids.
306	www.therapeuticsinc.com	9025 Balboa Ave., Suite 100, San Diego, CA 92123	Therapeutics is focused on dermatology-related areas of medicine and moving products from concept to clinical development with regulatory review and approval.
307	www.therapeuticsresearch.com	9025 Balboa Avenue, Suite 105, San Diego CA 92123	TCR specializes in research and development of drugs and devices for dermatology and skin care.
308	www.tocagen.com	3030 Bunker Hill St., #230, San Diego, CA 92109	Tocagen is a biopharmaceutical company focused on discovery, development and commercialization of products for the treatment of cancer.
309	www.tpims.org	3550 General Atomics Court, 2-129 San Diego, CA 92121-1122	Torrey Pines Institute for Molecular Studies is conducting biomedical research for the discovery of vaccines, treatments and cures for human disease and suffering, including multiple sclerosis, cancer, heart disease, diabetes, infectious diseases, pain and inflammation.
310	www.traconpharma.com	4510 Executive Drive, Suite 330, San Diego, CA 92121	Tracon Pharmaceuticals engages in identifying, developing, and commercializing therapeutics for cancer and angiogenesis.
311	www.traversathera.com	505 Coast Blvd South, Suite #405, La Jolla, CA 92037-4613	Traversa Therapeutics is focused on the discovery, development and commercialization of RNAi delivery technologies and on advancement of therapeutic programs for the treatment of leukemia and glioblastoma.
312	www.t-r-co.com	12255 El Camino Real, Suite 250, San Diego, CA 92130	Tissue Repair Company is focused on products promoting tissue repair. Its expertise is broadly based in gene therapy, growth factor biology, tissue regeneration and product development.

	COMPANY	ADDRESS	DESCRIPTION
313	www.trilinkbiotech.com	9955 Mesa Rim Road, San Diego, CA 92121	TriLink is focused on manufacturing of high quality oligo-nucleotides and nucleoside triphosphates at small and mid-scales.
314	www.triusrx.com	6310 Nancy Ridge Drive, Suite 101, San Diego, CA 92121	Trius is focused on development of antibacterial drugs for the treatment of infections caused by resistant bacteria.
315	www.trlusa.com	4540 Towne Centre Court, San Diego, California 92121	Tanabe Research Laboratories USA (TRL) is focused on small molecule drug discovery.
316	www.ultimatelab.com	5940 Pacific Mesa Court, Suite 209, San Diego, CA 92121	Ultimate Labs provides the convenient, efficient and professional environmental monitoring services and microbiological testing.
317	www.valasciences.com	3030 Bunker Hill, Suite 203, San Diego, CA 92109	Vala Sciences has developed technologies to enable information-rich measurements for fundamental research of cell functions.
318	www.validationsystems.com	5230 Carroll Canyon Road, Suite 118, San Diego, CA 92121	VSI is a full service validation contractor servicing the biotechnology, pharmaceutical, and medical device industries.
319	www.valormedical.com	6749 Top Gun Street, Suite 109, San Diego, CA 92121	Valor Medical's product, Neucrylate™ is formulated to meet the delivery requirements for treating cerebral berry aneurysm and coil salvage therapy.
320	www.vaxiion.com	11585 Sorrento Valley Road, Suite 105, San Diego, California, 92121	Vaxiion is focused on the design and development of drug-delivery technologies with special emphasis on targeted oncology therapeutics.
321	www.ventirx.com	12651 High Bluff Drive Suite 200 San Diego, CA 92130	VentiRx Pharmaceuticals develops novel medicines for treatment of cancer, infectious, respiratory, and autoimmune diseases.
322	www.verdezyne.com	2715 Loker Ave, Carlsbad, CA 92008	Verdezyne is focused on the design and synthesis of novel, diverse gene libraries for engineering of proteins, metabolic pathways, and microorganisms.
323	www.veruspharm.com	12671 High Bluff Drive, Ste 200, San Diego, CA 92130	Pediatric-oriented company dedicated to identifying, developing and delivering solutions to address the unmet medical needs of children.
324	www.vet-stem.com	12860 Danielson Court, Suite B, Poway, CA 92064	Vet-Stem provides a quick-turnaround laboratory service that enables veterinarians to utilize regenerative cells in animals.
325	www.vical.com	10390 Pacific Center Court, San Diego, California 92121	Vical is focused on development of biopharmaceutical products based on proprietary DNA delivery technologies for the prevention and treatment of life-threatening diseases.
326	www.vicsd.com	7522-7524 Clairmont Mesa Blvd. San Diego CA 92111	The Veterinary Imaging Center of San Diego is veterinary radioiodine therapy and outpatient imaging facility.
327	www.victorypharma.com	11682 El Camino Real Suite 250, San Diego, CA 92130	Victory Pharma is focused on development, commercialization, and marketing of prescription pharmaceutical products for treatment of pain and related conditions.
328	www.virapur.com	6160 Lusk Blvd., Suite C101, San Diego, CA 92121 USA	Virapur is a virus production and purification company, offering custom virus production and purification services.

	COMPANY	ADDRESS	DESCRIPTION
329	www.vistabiologicals.com	2120-C Las Palmas Drive, Carlsbad, CA 92009	Vista Biologicals Corporation is focused on process development in the area of animal cell culture, protein purification and pilot scale product production.
330	www.vlpbiotech.com	10835 Road to the Cure, Suite 155, San Diego, CA 92121 USA	VLP Biotech is focused on developing novel vaccine therapies for the treatment of infectious diseases and other disorders.
331	www.vp-scientific.com	9823 Pacific Heights Boulevard, Suite T, San Diego, CA 92121	V&P Scientific is making replicators and manifolds to fill, aspirate, evaporate, mix, dilute, transfer, assay, screen, macroarray, microarray, spot, blot and tissue culture wounding in, to and from microplates.
332	www.vrisd.org	3030 Bunker Hill St Ste 300, San Diego, CA 92109	Vaccine Research Institute of San Diego is focused on development of vaccines for diseases in which standard immunization protocols have not produced protective immunity.
333	www.vrphobia.com	6155 Cornerstone Court East, Suite 210, San Diego, CA 92121	The Virtual Reality Medical Center applies simulation technologies to treat patients with anxiety disorders, training, and enhancing various educational programs.
334	www.vrtx.com	11010 Torreyana Road, San Diego, CA 92121	Vertex product pipeline is focused on viral diseases, cystic fibrosis, inflammation, autoimmune diseases, cancer and pain.
335	www.whitelabs.com	7564 Trade Street, San Diego, CA 92121	White Labs cultures and distributes liquid yeast to brewers, distillers and wine makers.
336	www.zogenix.com	12671 High Bluff Drive, Suite 200, San Diego, CA 92130	Zogenix is focused on the development and commercialization of differentiated central nervous system and pain therapeutics.

Figure 1. Word frequency analysis depicting the San Diego biotech profile as a 'Word cloud'. The collective focus of the San Diego company-domain is on '*research*' and '*development*'. Secondary in ranks are '*drug*', '*diseases*', '*discovery*' and '*services*'. Tertiary in importance are the '*cancer*', '*novel*', '*pharmaceutical*', '*therapeutics*'. Lower in ranks are '*diagnostics*', '*clinical*', and '*medical*'.